HEINEMANN
STATE STUDIES

Uniquely
Arizona

James A. Corrick

Heinemann Library
Chicago, Illinois

© 2004 Heinemann Library
a division of Reed Elsevier Inc.
Chicago, Illinois

Customer Service   888-454-2279

Visit our website at www.heinemannlibrary.com

Designed by Heinemann Library
Printed in China by WKT Company Limited.

08 07 06 05 04
10 9 8 7 6 5 4 3 2 1

**Library of Congress
Cataloging-in-Publication Data**

Corrick, James A.
  Uniquely Arizona / James A. Corrick.
    p. cm. — (Heinemann state studies)
Summary: Examines what makes Arizona unique,
including its history, geography, people, culture,
and attractions.
Includes bibliographical references and index.
    ISBN 1-4034-4486-2 (HC library binding) —
ISBN 1-4034-4501-X (PB)
1. Arizona—Juvenile literature. [1. Arizona.]
I. Title. II. Series.
  F811.3.C66 2003
  979.1—dc21

                                    2003009433

Cover Pictures

Top (left to right) saguaro cactus in the
Sonoran Desert, Geronimo, Arizona state flag,
rodeo performer **Main** the Grand Canyon

Acknowledgments
Development and photo research by
BOOK BUILDERS LLC

The author and publishers are grateful to the following for permission to reproduce copyright
material:

Cover photographs by (top, L-R) George H. H.
Huey/Corbis; Bettmann/Corbis; Joseph Sohm/
Visions of America/Corbis; Jerry Cooke/Corbis;
(main) David Muench/Corbis

Title page (L-R): Michael Bisceglie/Earth Scenes;
Tom Till/Bachman/Photo Researchers; Contents
page Mickey Gibson/AnimalsAnimals; p. 5 James
Blank/Bruce Coleman Inc.; p. 6, Michael Bisceglie/
Earth Scenes; p. 7T, Linde Waidhofer/Alamy; p. 7B
George H.H. Huey/Corbis; pp. 8, 41, 45 maps by
IMA for Book Builders LLC; p. 10 Brand X/Alamy;
p. 11 Joseph Sohm/Visions of America/Corbis; pp.
12, 26 Andre Jenny/Alamy; p. 13T Zig Lesczcnvski/
Earth Scenes; p. 13B Steve Hamblin/Alamy; p. 14T
Mickey Gibson/AnimalsAnimals; p. 14B G. C. Kelley/
Photo Researchers; p. 15T George Andrejko/Arizona
Game and Fish Dept.; p. 15M Zig Lesczcnvski/
AnimalsAnimals; p. 15B Tom McHugh/Photo
Researchers; pp. 16T, 18 Courtesy Arizona Office of
Tourism; pp. 16M, 20, 31 Robert Harding Picture
Library Ltd/Alamy; p. 16B Ronald F. Thomas/Bruce
Coleman Inc.; p. 17 Tom Till/Alamy; p. 21 Bettmann/
Corbis; pp. 22, 23B George Jones/Photo Researchers;
p. 23T Arthur Schotz/Getty Images; p. 24 David
Muench/Corbis; p. 25 Index Stock/Alamy; p. 29
Bachman/Photo Researchers; p. 30 Jerry Cooke/
Corbis; p. 32 Momentum Creative Group/Alamy;
p. 33 Gordon E. Smith/Photo Researchers; p. 34 R.
Capozzelli/Heinemann Library; p. 36 Barry Gossage/
NBAE/Getty Images; p. 37T Courtesy University of
Arizona; p. 37B Courtesy of Arizona State University;
p. 38 Donald Specker/Earth Scenes; p. 39 Joseph
Sohm/Alamy; p. 40 Mark Newman/Bruce Coleman
Inc.; p. 42 Dinodia Photo Library/Alamy; p. 43
Donna Kenberry/Earth Scenes; p. 44 Lightworks
Media/Alamy.

Special thanks to Judith L. Moreillon of the University of Arizona for her expert comments in the
preparation of this book.

Every effort has been made to contact copyright
holders of any material reproduced in this book.
Any omissions will be rectified in subsequent print-
ings if notice is given to the publisher.

Some words are shown in bold, **like this.**
You can find out what they mean by looking
in the glossary.

Contents

Uniquely Arizona

There is no other place exactly like Arizona. It is unique. To be unique is to be different from everything else in the world. The state is located in the southwestern part of the United States—east of California and west of New Mexico.

When people think of Arizona, they often picture the Grand Canyon. It is just one of the state's many natural wonders. Others include the Painted Desert, the Petrified Forest, and the Meteor Crater. Arizona is also a state with year-round sunshine. Cities such as Yuma and Tucson enjoy more than 350 sunny days each year.

ORIGIN OF THE STATE'S NAME

No one knows how Arizona got its name. It may come from a Native American word *aleh-zon,* meaning "place of the small spring." The name may be from the Spanish *arida zona,* or dry land.

MAJOR CITIES

Most of Arizona's 5 million people live in cities. Phoenix, the state capital, has a population of 1.3 million, making it the largest city in the state and the largest capital city in the nation. Phoenix is named for a legendary bird that is said to rise from its ashes every 500 years. The name is fitting. Phoenix is located on the site of an ancient Hohokam settlement. The Hohokam, a Native American people, lived in the Salt River Valley until about 600 years ago, when they suddenly disappeared. They left behind their homes and the many canals and ditches they dug to bring water to their fields.

In 1867 Jack Swilling, an American who came to Arizona after the **Civil War** (1861–1865), decided to encourage farming by rebuilding the old canals. Within six months, his company was providing water to dozens of farms. In 1870 settlers in the area started the town they called Phoenix, because it, too, rose on the ruins of an earlier people.

Over the years, the people of Phoenix have replaced the old canals with more modern **irrigation** systems. With a steady supply of water and the invention of air conditioning, Phoenix has become one of the fastest-growing cities in the nation. From 1950 to 2000, its population has grown from 106,000 to more than 1.3 million people.

Southeast of Phoenix is Tucson. It is the second-largest city in the state, with almost a half million people. The Spanish founded Tucson in 1775 as a fort. The city's age has earned it the nickname "Old **Pueblo.**" Tucson also calls itself as the astronomy capital of the world. In the mountains near Tucson are some two dozen telescopes that explore everything from the age of the universe to the makeup of the sun.

Tucson is home to the University of Arizona.

Almost directly north of Phoenix is Flagstaff. Flagstaff has a population of 57,000 people. At 7,000 feet above sea level, it is one of the highest cities in the nation. The city's name comes from the flagpole, or flagstaff, that early settlers put up on July 4, 1876, to celebrate the 100th birthday of the United States. Many tourists come to Flagstaff to visit Native American sites, ski resorts, and landmarks, such as the Grand Canyon and the Petrified Forest.

Arizona's Geography and Climate

Arizona's land and **climate** vary from north to south. The land can be dry deserts or snow-covered mountains. The climate is affected by the **elevation** of the land.

LAND

Arizona has two main regions—the Colorado Plateau in the north and the Basin and Range in the south. The Colorado Plateau is a highland broken in places by the San Francisco Peaks and the White Mountains. **Canyons** and **mesas** also cut through the plateau. The largest and best known is the Grand Canyon.

Along the southern edge of the Colorado Plateau are huge rock walls nearly 2,000 feet high. Known as the Mogollon Rim, these walls stretch for nearly 200 miles from central Arizona to the Mogollon Mountains in southwestern New Mexico.

The Basin and Range region in southern Arizona contains rugged mountain ranges that run from northwest to southeast. Between the mountains are broad, flat valleys known

Arizona's highest peak is Humphreys Peak. It stands 12,633 feet above sea level.

as basins. Those valleys are narrower in the northern part of the region and wider and more fertile toward the center of the region.

The Colorado River is Arizona's most important river. It enters the state from Utah and winds west and south to form the state's border with California.

CLIMATE

Two words sum up Arizona's climate—hot and dry. About two-thirds of the state is desert. A desert receives less than ten inches of **precipitation** a year. Not every place in Arizona is as dry as its deserts.

Monument Valley in the Colorado Plateau is mostly flat and dry, but in winter, precipitation often falls as snow.

The Sonoran Giant Cacti

The saguaro **cactus** is found only in the Sonoran Desert. It is a plant that grows so slowly that it can take ten years to add an inch to its height. It may take a saguaro more than 50 years to grow arms. Many of the cacti in the Sonoran Desert are 30 feet tall and have many branches, or arms. Saguaro cacti do not grow anywhere else in the United States.

The mountains receive about 25 to 30 inches of precipitation a year. They are also 20°F to 30°F cooler than lower land nearby. As the winds push air up over those mountains, the air gets colder. Cold air holds less water than warm air. So whatever moisture is in the air falls over the mountains as rain or snow.

The desert cities of Phoenix and Yuma are much drier and hotter than the central mountain city of Flagstaff, whose climate resembles that of many eastern cities.

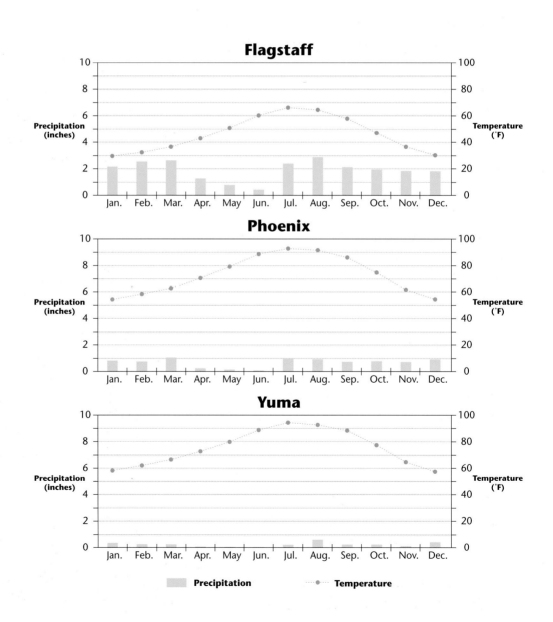

Famous Firsts

NATIVE AMERICAN FIRSTS

Oraibi, in northern Arizona, is the oldest settlement in the United States. The Hopi have occupied the town for almost 900 years.

Native American **reservations** take up 25 percent of Arizona's land, more than any other state.

Arizona's Navajo reservation covers approximately 25,000 square miles, an area about the size of West Virginia. It is the largest reservation in the country.

The Navajo's Rough Rock School, founded in 1966, is the first in the nation to be run by Native Americans. It is also the first to use a Native American language for instruction. Rough Rock has served as a model for other Native American schools in the United States.

Kitt Peak National Observatory, founded in 1958, is the first national observatory in the United States and has the world's largest collection of optical telescopes.

ASTRONOMY FIRSTS

In January 1930 Clyde W. Tombaugh, an astronomer at the Lowell Observatory at Flagstaff, discovered the planet Pluto.

In July 1978 astronomers at the U.S. Naval Observatory at Flagstaff discovered that Pluto has a moon. Its discoverers named it Charon.

Kitt Peak National Observatory, west of Tucson, has the world's largest solar

In addition to hummingbirds, Ramsey Canyon is home to 170 other types of birds.

telescope. The telescope, which is 780 feet long, is used to study the sun. Its length is necessary to produce a clear, sharp image.

OTHER FIRSTS

Ramsey Canyon, southeast of Tucson, is the hummingbird capital of the world. During the spring and summer, fourteen kinds of hummingbirds live here. A hummingbird is a small bird that flaps its wings so fast that it hovers in the air like a helicopter. The San Pedro River runs through the canyon. Its water attracts the birds.

The town of Fountain Hills, near Phoenix, has built the world's tallest fountain. Every hour for 30 minutes, the fountain shoots water 560 feet into the air.

Prescott is the home of the nation's oldest rodeo. It was first held in 1888.

In 1988 the Telephone Pioneers of America Park opened in Phoenix. It is the first park designed for the physically challenged. Among many other features, it has a wheelchair-accessible playground.

Palo Verde **nuclear** power plant, 50 miles west of Phoenix, is the largest in the United States. A nuclear power plant produces electricity by splitting **atoms.** Palo Verde serves 4 million people in Arizona, California, New Mexico, and Texas.

Arizona's State Symbols

ARIZONA STATE FLAG

In 1917 Arizona lawmakers approved the state's flag. The thirteen rays of red and gold on the top half of the flag represent the first thirteen states in the United States. The rays also show a setting sun. The setting sun is a sign that Arizona is a western state, because the sun sets in the west. The copper star highlights the state's copper mines, which drew many people to Arizona. Since 1910 it has been the nation's largest producer of copper.

STATE MOTTO: *DITAT DEUS*

Since 1912 Arizona's state motto has been *Ditat Deus,* Latin for "God enriches." Arizonans feel rich in their state's mix of cultures, land, and such natural resources as copper, gold, and silver.

The red and gold on the flag are a reminder of the colors on the flags Spanish explorers carried into what is now Arizona in 1560. The blue is the same shade found on the U.S. flag.

STATE NICKNAME: GRAND CANYON STATE

Arizona's Grand Canyon is larger and deeper than any other canyon in the world. In honor of this unique natural feature, Arizona adopted the nickname "Grand Canyon State."

The state seal appears on official state documents.

ARIZONA STATE SEAL

Arizona's seal was adopted in 1912, the year Arizona became the 48th state. The seal shows figures and objects associated with Arizona. Among them are a miner with a pick and shovel, grazing cattle, irrigated fields, and tall mountains.

STATE SONG: "ARIZONA MARCH SONG"

The "Arizona March Song" became the state song in 1919. Four years earlier Margaret Rowe Clifford wrote the words, and Maurice Blumenthal set those words to music.

"Arizona March Song"

Come to this land of sunshine
To this land where life is young.
Where the wide, wide world is waiting,
The songs that will now be sung.
Where the golden sun is flaming
Into warm, white shining day,
And the sons of men are blazing
Their priceless right of way.

Come stand beside the rivers
Within our valley broad.
Stand here with heads uncovered,
In the presence of our God!
While all around, about us
The brave, unconquered band,
As guardians and landmarks
The giant mountains stand.

Not alone for gold and silver
Is Arizona great.
But with graves of heroes sleeping,
All the land is consecrate!
O, come and live beside us
However far ye roam
Come and help us build up temples
And name those temples "home."

Chorus
Sing the song that's in your hearts
Sing of the great Southwest,
Thank God, for Arizona
In splendid sunshine dressed.
For thy beauty and thy grandeur,
For thy regal robes so sheen
We hail thee Arizona
Our goddess and our queen.

In the spring the palo verde is covered with small gold flowers.

STATE TREE: PALO VERDE

The palo verde became the state tree in 1954. The tree, whose name is Spanish for "green stick," has a green bark. It grows in the desert and foothills of Arizona.

STATE FLOWER: SAGUARO CACTUS

In 1931 the saguaro cactus blossom became the state flower. The waxy blossoms, which bloom in May and June, turn into red fruits in July.

The saguaro cactus blossom opens at night.

STATE BIRD: CACTUS WREN

In 1931 the cactus wren became the state bird. The wren makes its home in the southern and western parts of the state. It got its name because it nests in cacti. The plant's sharp needles offer protection from animals that hunt birds for food.

The noises that the cactus wren makes sound as if it were a car having trouble starting.

STATE MAMMAL: RINGTAIL

In 1985 the Arizona Game and Fish Department asked Arizona school children to select a state mammal. The winner was the ringtail, or ringtail cat. In 1986 it became the official state mammal. The ringtail, a shy creature, is related to the raccoon. Its tail makes up half of the length of its body.

Young ringtails are born blind and have soft white fur.

Apache trout live in small mountain streams and grow to be about 22 inches long.

STATE FISH: APACHE TROUT

In 1986 Arizona schoolchildren chose the Apache or Arizona trout as the state fish. This fish, which is found only in Arizona, is **endangered.**

STATE AMPHIBIAN: ARIZONA TREEFROG

In 1986 the Arizona treefrog became the state amphibian. Native to Arizona, these frogs, which are no more than two inches long, live in the central mountains of the state. Sticky pads on the frog's feet make it an excellent tree climber.

The Arizona treefrog is mostly active at night and eats only insects.

STATE REPTILE: RIDGE-NOSED RATTLESNAKE

In 1986 the ridge-nosed rattlesnake became the state reptile. Arizona has more types of rattlesnakes than any other state. One of the smallest is the ridge-nosed, which weighs only three to four ounces. This snake lives in the southeastern mountains of Arizona.

The ridge-nosed rattlesnake eats lizards and other small snakes.

Petrified wood often shows what the inside of these once-living trees looked like.

STATE FOSSIL: PETRIFIED WOOD

Arizona officially named petrified wood as its state **fossil** in 1988. These fossils were trees 200 million years ago. Over a long period of time, the wood became petrified—that is, it became as hard as a rock. Most petrified wood in Arizona is found in the Petrified Forest in the northern part of the state.

Turquoise has been used for centuries in Native American jewelry

STATE GEMSTONE: TURQUOISE

Since 1974 turquoise has been Arizona's official gemstone. It has been an important gemstone in Arizona throughout history. Prehistoric ancestors of the Hualapai Indians mined turquoise in the Cerbat Mountains north of present-day Kingman and Interstate 40. Today, turquoise can be found all over the state.

STATE NECKWEAR: BOLA TIE

In 1971 Arizona bccamc thc only statc with an official neckwear, the bola tie. Invented in Arizona, the bola is a thin leather string whose ends pass through a clasp, usually made of silver and turquoise.

The bola tie gots its name because it looks like a South American hunting weapon, called the boleadoras.

Arizona's History and People

The story of Arizona stretches thousands of years into the past. Arizona has been the home to hunters, farmers, soldiers, miners, and business people, among others.

NATIVE PEOPLES

People have been living in what is now Arizona for about 8,000 years. Around 2,300 years ago, the eastern mountains were home to the Mogollon people, who were hunters and gatherers. At about the same time, the Anasazi moved into Arizona from the north and the Hohokam from the south.

At first, the Anasazi lived in villages and grew corn, beans, and squash. About 1,200 years ago, they began to build structures that resemble modern apartment houses. About 300

The largest of the Anasazi cliff dwellings may have housed around 1,000 people.

Once a nomadic tribe, the Navajo lived in brush shelters called hogans. Today, many Navajo continue to live in the traditional hogans on reservations east of the Grand Canyon in Arizona.

years later, they began to carve whole towns into the sides of cliffs. The Hohokam were also farmers. They used **irrigation** to turn parts of the Sonoran Desert into farmland.

All three peoples disappeared more than 700 years ago. No one knows what happened to them, but some scientists think **drought,** disease, or war may have ended their way of life.

The present-day Hopi of northern Arizona may be descendants of the Anasazi, and the Akimel O'odham (Pima) and the Tohono O'odham (Papago) of southern Arizona may be descendants of the Hohokam. Apaches and Navajos came to Arizona around 700 years ago. The Apaches settled in central and southern Arizona, and the Navajo settled in northeastern Arizona.

ARRIVALS FROM SPAIN AND MEXICO

In 1540 the Spanish came to what is now Arizona in search of the legendary Seven Golden Cities of **Cibola.** In 1539 Fray Marcos de Niza, a Spanish **missionary,** claimed that he saw Cibola. The following year, Francisco Vásquez de Coronado led an expedition through southeastern Arizona in hopes of finding it.

When Coronado was unable to find cities of gold, the Spanish lost interest in Arizona until the 1680s, when Catholic missionaries moved to the area. In 1752 the Spanish set up a fort at Tubac, about 40 miles south of present-day Tucson, to protect the missionaries from Native Americans who resented the newcomers. Farmers and other settlers from Mexico followed the soldiers to Arizona.

WAR WITH MEXICO

In 1821 Mexico won its freedom from Spain, and Arizona became part of the new nation. In 1846 the United States invaded Mexico because of a border dispute. The United States won the war, and Mexico had to give up a vast territory called the Mexican Cession. It included California and much of modern-day Arizona, Nevada, New Mexico, and Utah.

ARIZONA TERRITORY

In 1849 the U.S. army set up Camp Calhoun near present-day Yuma. It was the first of a series of forts that protected U.S. settlers from conflicts with Native Americans. In 1851 the army built a road across northern Arizona. Flagstaff and Williams were among the towns that grew along the road. By 1860 approximately 2,500 U.S. settlers were living in Arizona.

The Gadsden Purchase

In 1853 the United States paid Mexico $10 million for parts of what is now southern Arizona and New Mexico. The territory was called the Gadsden Purchase after James Gadsden, the U.S. ambassador to Mexico. He arranged the deal. Americans wanted the land for a railroad across the southern part of the country.

Arizona During the Civil War

When the **Civil War** began in 1861, many in Arizona sided with the **Confederacy.** In February 1862 Confederate troops arrived in the territory, and on April 15 they fought U.S. soldiers at Picacho Peak. It was the westernmost battle of the war. Although the Confederates won the battle, Arizona remained a U.S. territory.

The settlers clashed with the Apaches, who **resented** the invasion of their land. The constant fighting slowed but did not stop the arrival of more Americans. Most of them came to mine for copper, gold, and silver. By 1880 the Southern Pacific Railroad had linked the territory to the rest of the country. New towns sprang up along the rail lines.

Hundreds of people on both sides died as a result of the conflict between the Apaches and the Americans. Other Native Americans in Arizona, the Yavapai and the Navajo in particular, also fought the newcomers. There was no single battle that ended the war. Still, by the 1890s most Native Americans were living on government-run **reservations.**

STATEHOOD

By the early 1900s Arizona's population reached 200,000, and many people in the territory were eager for statehood. On February 14, 1912, Arizona became the 48th state. It was the last continental territory to become a state.

The Navajo Code Talkers

During **World War II** (1941–1945) the Japanese were able to figure out the coded radio messages sent by the U.S. army. The military needed a new, unbreakable code.

A group of Navajo marines, known as code talkers, developed one based on their native language. It stumped the Japanese, a service about which Native Americans are proud.

FAMOUS PEOPLE

Eusebio Francisco Kino (1645–1711), Catholic **missionary.** Born in Segno, Italy, Kino led the first of 40 expeditions into Arizona in 1681. He explored the sources of the Colorado and Gila rivers and founded thirteen missions.

Geronimo (1829–1908), Apache leader. Born in northern Mexico, Germonimo attacked U.S. settlements in 1876, after 4,000 Apaches were forced onto the San Carlos Reservation in eastern Arizona. The U.S. army was unable to capture the Apache leader until 1886. After serving time in a Florida prison, he settled in Oklahoma.

Geronimo was the leader of the last band of Native Americans who fought the U.S. government.

Wyatt Earp (1848–1929), law enforcement officer. Born in Monmouth, Illinois, Wyatt joined his brothers Virgil and Morgan as **marshals** in Tombstone in 1878. The Earps fought the Clantons, a ranching family, for political control of the town. On October 6, 1881, the Earps won a battle that left three Clantons dead. The Gunfight at the O.K. Corral, as it became known, came to represent the violence of Arizona's territorial days.

Louis Tewanima (1877–1969), long-distance runner. Born on the Hopi reservation, Twanima won a silver medal in the 1912 Olympics in Stockholm, Sweden, for the 10,000-meter run. He set a U.S. record that stood for 32 years.

Barry Goldwater (1909–1998), politician. Born in Phoenix, Goldwater, a **Republican,** served in the U.S. Senate for more than 30 years. Goldwater tried to decrease the power of the U.S. government and increase state and local control.

A photograph of the flag-raising at Iwo Jima has been made into a statue. It stands in Arlington National Cemetery near Washington, D.C. Hayes is the figure on the far left.

Raul Castro (1916–), politician. Born in Cananea, Mexico, Castro moved to Arizona in 1926 and became a U.S. citizen. A **Democrat,** he served as a state judge and later ambassador to El Salvador and Colombia. In 1975 Castro became the first Mexican American governor of a U.S. state.

Ira Hamilton Hayes (1923–1955), war hero. Hayes was born on the Akimel O'odham Gila River Reservation. As a marine during **World War II,** he helped raise the U.S. flag on the Japanese-held island of Iwo Jima in February 1945.

R.C. Gorman (1931–), artist. Born on the Navajo Reservation, Gorman's paintings have appeared in many art galleries and museums, including New York City's Metropolitan Museum of Art.

John McCain (1936–), war hero and politician. Born in the Panama Canal Zone, McCain was a navy pilot who spent more than five years as a prisoner of war during the **Vietnam War.** After retiring from the navy, McCain, a **Republican,** moved to Arizona, and in 1986 won a seat in the U.S. Senate. He ran for president in 2000.

To draw attention to his cause, César Chávez often refused to eat for one or two weeks.

César Chávez (1927–1993), labor leader. Born near Yuma, Chávez founded the National Farm Workers Association (NFWA) in 1962. It was the first successful farm workers' union in U.S. history. In 1965 Chávez led a five-year **strike** and **boycott** of grape growers in California. It rallied millions of people in support of field-workers.

Sandra Day O'Connor (1930–), U.S. Supreme Court justice. Born in El Paso, Texas, O'Connor was raised on a ranch in southeastern Arizona. A former state judge, she became the first woman to be appointed to the U.S. Supreme Court in 1981.

Sandra Day O'Connor was appointed to the Arizona State Senate in 1969 and served as a legislator there until 1974, when she was elected a trial judge for Maricopa County.

The Grand Canyon

The Grand Canyon, the largest canyon in the world, slices through 277 miles of northern Arizona and runs from the Utah border to the Nevada border. Its steep walls are four to eighteen miles apart, and in places, they drop more than a mile to the canyon floor.

A NATURAL WONDER

The Grand Canyon, which was carved by the Colorado River, is the result of water **erosion.** Scientists are not sure exactly how long it took to create the canyon, but they estimate it was between 1 and 4 million years.

The walls of the Grand Canyon form a record of the earth that stretches more than four million years.

At the canyon's bottom are the remains of ancient mountains. Along the steep sides of the canyon, layers of rock reveal how the area's temperature and precipitation have changed over the centuries. Millions of years ago, the area was under water.

DISCOVERING THE CANYON

Native Americans have lived in and around the Grand Canyon for at least 8,000 years. In 1540 the first Spanish explorers arrived under the command of

García López de Cárdenas. Then, in 1869, the Americans came. Geologist John Wesley Powell led ten men on the first recorded expedition through the canyon.

Around 277 of the Colorado River's nearly 1,500 miles flow through the Grand Canyon.

Few people knew much about the Grand Canyon until Powell wrote a book about his experiences in 1875. Many got their first look at the canyon through the photographs of Timothy O'Sullivan, a member of an 1871 Grand Canyon expedition.

In the 1880s thousands of visitors came to see the canyon for themselves. They arrived by stagecoach until 1901, when the Grand Canyon Railway opened. It remains in operation to this day.

NATIONAL PARK

By 1915 about 100,000 people were visiting the Grand Canyon each year. It was such a popular attraction that Congress made the canyon a national park in 1919. By doing so, lawmakers were able to protect the canyon from companies eager to mine its resources. In 1975 Congress added more land to the park, which now covers more than a million acres.

Today nearly five million tourists from all over the world visit the Grand Canyon every year. Some hike or ride mules along trails that lead to the canyon floor, while others fly over the canyon in airplanes and helicopters.

Arizona's State Government

In 1911 Arizona adopted a state constitution. Like the U.S. Constitution, it sets up a state government that is divided into three branches or divisions: legislative, executive, and judicial. Like the U.S. Constitution, it also guarantees certain rights, such as freedom of speech and religion. Arizona's government is based in Phoenix, the state capital.

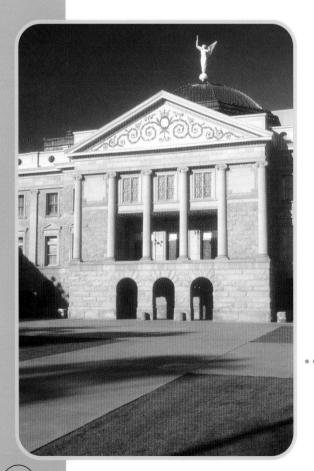

LEGISLATIVE BRANCH

Arizona's legislature makes laws for the state. It is divided into two houses, a house of representatives with 60 members and a senate with 30 members. Lawmakers serve for two years.

The legislature meets for 100 days every year, beginning on the second Monday in January to propose new **bills.** For a bill to become law, it must be approved by a majority (more than half of the members) in each house and signed by the gover-

Originally all three branches of government were housed in the capitol building. Today each branch has its own building.

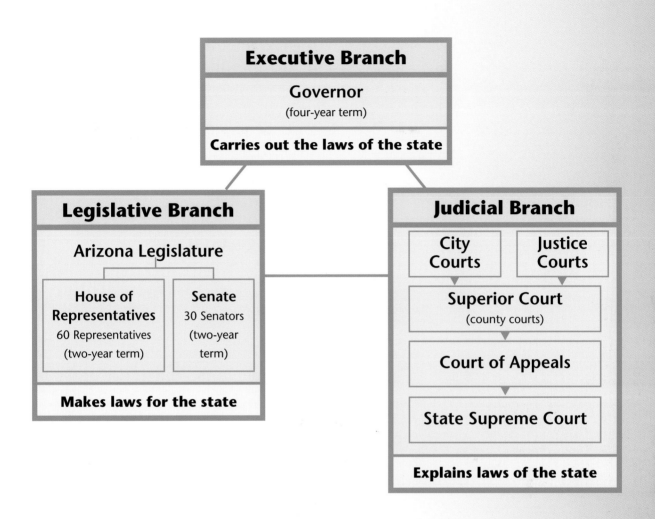

Executive Branch

Governor
(four-year term)

Carries out the laws of the state

Legislative Branch

Arizona Legislature

House of Representatives	Senate
60 Representatives (two-year term)	30 Senators (two-year term)

Makes laws for the state

Judicial Branch

City Courts	Justice Courts

Superior Court
(county courts)

Court of Appeals

State Supreme Court

Explains laws of the state

nor. If the governor **vetoes** a bill, the legislature can still pass it into law if it has the approval of two-thirds of each house.

EXECUTIVE BRANCH

The executive branch enforces the laws the legislature passes. The state's top executive is the governor. The governor appoints the heads of state agencies, such as the Department of Public Safety (state police), and oversees their work. Each year the governor also draws up a state budget, which must be approved by the legislature.

Arizona voters elect five members of the executive branch—the governor, **secretary of state, treasurer,**

Governor Janet Napolitano also served as Arizona's attorney general.

attorney general, and **superintendent of public instruction.** Each may serve two four-year terms in a row. Unlike most states, Arizona does not have a lieutenant governor. Instead, the secretary of state serves as acting governor when the governor is away.

JUDICIAL BRANCH

The judicial branch interprets state laws. That is, the courts decide how the laws apply to a particular case.

In Arizona, city courts and courts run by justices of the peace try people for **misdemeanors.** The justice of the peace courts also handle **civil suits** of less than $10,000. Voters in countywide elections choose justices of the peace. Each serves a four-year term.

The state superior court, which has judges in each of Arizona's fifteen counties, tries those charged with **felonies,** such as murder or burglary. It also grants divorces and handles civil suits. The judges also hear appeals from lower courts. Either side in a case can appeal a decision reached in a lower court. Superior court judges may uphold the decision or overturn it. In all but two counties, superior court judges are elected to a four-year term.

Superior court decisions may also be appealed. They may be sent to the state court of appeals or the state supreme court. The five justices on the state supreme court have the final say. The governor appoints each to a six-year term.

Arizona's Culture

Many groups of people have made their home in Arizona. The three largest are Anglo-Americans, Mexican Americans, and Native Americans. An Anglo-American is anyone whose ancestors came from a European country other than Spain. Many Mexican Americans are descended from the Native Americans of Mexico and the Spanish. Fifteen Native American peoples live in Arizona. Together, these groups helped to create Arizona's unique culture, or way of life.

MUSIC

Arizona has been deeply influenced by the music of Mexican Americans. *Mariachis* developed in central Mexico in the 1800s. Mexicans brought the music to Arizona almost immediately. Mariachis are musical groups that play string instruments, such as violins and guitars. Some groups add trumpets.

Mariachis play everything from old Mexican folksongs to newly composed music. Each year in August the city of Chandler throws the

Mariachis can be a group as small as three musicians or as large as twelve.

The Waila of the Tohono O'odham

The *waila* combines the Native American group Tohono O'odham traditional dance music with the polka, a dance popular in Poland. Waila bands use accordions, drums, saxophones, and guitars. The music is sometimes called "chicken scratch," because performers originally kicked their heels back and up. From a distance, they looked like chickens scratching in the dirt. Modern waila dancers move in a smooth, gliding motion. Tucson holds a waila festival every year in May.

Fiesta de Chandler. There, top mariachis play. The fiesta also features *folklorico*, or Mexican folk dancing.

Every year Arizona has many other music festivals that celebrate the musical contributions of other cultures to the state. Jazz on the Rocks, which began in 1981, is held in Sedona. The festival's name comes from its outdoor setting, a circle of red rocks. Jazz originated with African American musicians in the early 1900s. They used trumpets, trombones, clarinets, and other musical instruments to improvise, change, or make up music on the spur of the moment. Today Jazz on the Rocks is held in the fall and draws its audience and musicians from all over the world, including Mexico.

RODEO

Arizona has its share of cattle ranches and cowboys. This part of the state's culture is celebrated in its many rodeos. Originally the rodeo was a place where cowhands could show off the skills they used in their work with cattle. These and other ranch duties gave rise to such major rodeo events as calf roping, **bronco** and bull riding, and steer wrestling.

Some rodeo performers still work on ranches, but many are professional athletes, who train long and hard.

The Arizona rodeo season swings into gear in February with major rodeos in Goodyear and Tucson and ends in October in Wilcox and Kingman. Each of these events runs two to three days. The Tucson rodeo is known as *La Fiesta de los Vaqueros,* the Celebration of the Cowboys.

THE OSTRICH FESTIVAL

Though not a rodeo, a festival at Chandler celebrates a new addition to Arizona ranches: the ostrich. It is the only ostrich festival in the United States. Ostriches thrive in Arizona's dry warm climate, which is similar to that in their African homeland. Ostrich races are the highlights of the festival. An ostrich can run up to 25 miles an hour, even when carrying a rider or pulling a wagon.

FAIRS

Fairs are meeting places for people of different cultures. The largest is the Arizona State Fair, which is held in Phoenix each fall. There, visitors find amusement park rides, concerts, and contests of every kind. There are chili cook-offs and contests to see who can make the tastiest pie or jelly made from cactus fruit. The fair also has special days honoring Arizona's Mexican Americans and Native Americans.

The Navajo Nation Fair is held at Window Rock each September.

Another of Arizona's fairs, the Navajo Nation Fair, plays an important part in keeping Navajo traditions alive. The Navajo perform traditional dances and cook special dishes. There is even a race with wild horses.

Arizona's Food

Arizonans eat all kinds of foods, but Mexican dishes are especially popular. Mexican cooks use beans, chicken, beef, and chilies (small, hot fruits, also known as chili peppers). They often wrap these foods in tortilla, which is flat, circular bread made from flour or corn. Tortilla-wrapped dishes include burritos, **enchiladas,** and chimichangas.

Arizona's Mexican Food

Mexican food is hot and spicy because of the red and green chilies that go into almost every dish. Cooks, for instance, mix chilies with onions and tomatoes to make salsa. Salsa is also used as a sauce on burritos and other dishes and as a dip for corn chips.

Arizona foods are distinctly southwestern with tacos, enchilladas, refried beans, and salsa. Chilies often spice up a relatively mild dish.

Arizona Chili

Always have an adult work the stove top for you!

Ingredients

1 pound of ground beef

1 can (15 ounces) pinto beans

1 can (15 ounces) of whole
   tomatoes

1 can (8 ounces) of tomato sauce

1 can (3 ounces) diced green chilies

2 cups of chopped onion (**Always
   have an adult do the cutting for you!**)

3 tablespoons of chili powder

1 teaspoon of garlic powder

Directions

Brown the beef and drain off excess fat. Add beans, tomatoes, tomato sauce, green chiles, and onions. Mix and then add chili powder and garlic powder. Bring to a boil. Reduce heat, cover, and cook slowly for 30 minutes.

The chimichanga is native to Arizona. A cook prepares this dish by mixing beef or chicken with chilies before wrapping the mix in a tortilla. The chimichanga is then deep fried until it is crispy. It is usually served with salsa or sour cream on top.

Arizona chili is a popular stew that can be made with a variety of ingredients. Everyone has a special recipe.

Arizona's Folklore and Legends

People in Arizona tell many stories about their state. One of those people is Dolan Ellis. He has been Arizona's official balladeer since 1967. A balladeer sings the kind of song that tells a story. No other state has its own balladeer.

Arizona has many other storytellers who enjoy sharing their tales. Some are true stories. Many others are legends or folklore, stories that have been passed from one generation to the next. Each of these tales reflects the Arizona experience.

THE BLUEBIRD AND THE COYOTE

Arizona's Native Americans have many stories about the desert and its creatures. The Akimel O'odham people tell of how the bluebird and the coyote got their colors.

Bluebird was an ugly colorless bird until it found a beautiful blue lake. For three mornings in a row, the bird bathed in the lake, while singing a song. On the fourth morning, it lost all its feathers. By the following day the bird had new feathers, and they were as blue as the lake.

Coyote hid in the bushes watching the changes in Bluebird. When he saw Bluebird's new color, he wanted to be the same shade of blue. So Bluebird taught Coyote the song and told him to bathe in the lake. For three mornings Coyote jumped into the blue water, singing. On the fourth morning he lost his hair. The next day his hair was as blue as the lake.

Coyote, excited by the change, kept looking at his shadow to see if it, too, was blue. He was so busy checking the color of his shadow that he ran into a stump. He fell and kept rolling on the ground until he was no longer blue but a dusty brown. From then on, all coyotes have been dust colored.

THE LOST DUTCHMAN MINE

Arizona has many stories of lost treasures and lost gold or silver mines. The most famous lost mine is the Lost Dutchman Mine. It was owned by two prospectors who many people thought were Dutch. However, Jacob Waltz and Jacob Weiser really were German.

In the 1870s the two men were among the many prospectors who flocked to Florence, a town halfway between Tucson and Phoenix, in search of precious metals. Waltz and Weiser always had pouches bulging with gold nuggets but would not tell anyone where they found the gold. All they would say was that it came from the Superstition Mountains north of Florence.

After Weiser died Waltz moved to Phoenix. In 1891, as he lay dying, he told his housekeeper how to find the mine. He said that a stone cliff looked over it and that the sun shone on the gold at sunset. He ended by telling her that three red hills lay beyond the mine. She never found his treasure nor has anyone else. Today people still search for the Lost Dutchman Mine.

Arizona's Sports Teams

Sports are a big part of life in Arizona. The state has a number of professional and college teams.

PROFESSIONAL SPORTS

Arizona's oldest professional team is the Phoenix Suns basketball team. The Suns began playing in the National Basketball Association (NBA) in 1968 and have made it to the play-offs several times. They have played in the NBA finals twice but lost both times. Their loss to the Boston Celtics in Game 5 of the 1976 finals is one of the most famous games in NBA history. The game was tied at the end of regular play, and the two teams battled it out through three overtime periods before the Celtics finally won.

The state's newest professional team is a baseball team, the Arizona Diamondbacks. The Diamondbacks played their first game in 1998. Only three years later, in 2001, the team won the World Series after Luis Gonzales hit a single in the bottom of the ninth inning of the seventh and final game.

Arizona is also home to the Women's National Basketball Association (WNBA) team, the Phoenix Mercury. In the team's first two years, 1997 and 1998, it made

Penny Hardaway pulls up for a jump shot against the Orlando Magic at the America West Arena.

the play-offs for the WNBA championship. Phoenix also has an NFL team, the Arizona Cardinals, and an NHL team, the Coyotes.

COLLEGE SPORTS

Arizona's two major state universities have successful sports programs. In Tucson the University of Arizona, whose nickname is the Wildcats, shines in men's basketball. The Wildcats have thrilled fans by going to the National Collegiate Athletic Association (NCAA) tournament nineteen times in a row and by winning the National Championship in 1997. During the past fifteen years, the University of Arizona has won more games than any other NCAA team in the country.

The University of Arizona basketball team plays its home games at the McKale Center.

Arizona State University, located in Tempe, is home to one of the most successful women's gymnastics teams in the country. Since the team began competing in 1976, it has won 279 meets, almost three-quarters of its competitions. The team has gone to the NCAA National Tournament fifteen out of the past eighteen years.

Arizona State University has a long history of athletic achievement and draws fans from all over the state.

Arizona's Businesses and Products

Mining, farming and ranching, and tourism are some of the state's major industries.

MINING

Mining is one of Arizona's major industries. Arizona has been the number-one producer of copper in the United States since 1910. Arizona's copper mines contribute more than $10 billion each year to the state's $155 billion income. There is a large market for copper today. The average house in the United States has more than 400 pounds of copper in it. Computers, electrical wiring, and water pipes are all made of copper, at least in part. Since 1963 Americans have installed enough copper pipes in their buildings to circle the earth 200 times.

FARMING AND RANCHING

Farming and ranching contribute more than $6 billion a year to the state's income. Lettuce is Arizona's top crop.

Arizona's copper miners must dig out 3 tons, or 6,000 pounds, of rock to get 10 pounds of copper.

Mild temperatures around Yuma allow farmers there to grow lettuce in the winter rather than the summer. Yuma farmers produce almost all the winter lettuce in the United States. Yuma and the area around Phoenix also attract lemon, orange, and other citrus growers. Lemons are Arizona's largest citrus crop. The state produces 135,000 tons of lemons, almost a fifth of all lemons eaten in the United States.

Certain types of cotton need a long, hot, dry growing season, much like the summers in southern Arizona. The region produces enough cotton to make a pair of jeans for every person in the country.

TOURISM

The biggest industry in Arizona is tourism. About 150 million visitors annually fuel a $30-billion-a-year business. Twenty percent of all jobs in Arizona are in the tourism industry. From October through April, southern Arizona draws people from colder climates with daytime temperatures around 60 and 70 degrees.

OTHER ARIZONA BUSINESSES

Arizona has a large number of other industries. Intel, the top manufacturer of the **microprocessor,** has an assembly plant and office that handles worldwide sales in Chandler. In Tucson, Sunquest is the number-one producer of software to help doctors identify and treat illnesses.

Attractions and Landmarks

Arizona offers visitors many things to see and do besides a trip to the Grand Canyon. Every part of the state has its natural wonders, state and national parks, museums, and historic buildings.

NORTHERN ARIZONA

Hoover Dam is located in northwestern Arizona along the Nevada border. This huge mountain of concrete spans the Colorado River. It is more than 726 feet high and is longer than the Empire State Building in New York City is tall. The dam supplies electricity to Arizona, Nevada, and California and helps control flooding of the Colorado River. The waters backed up behind Hoover Dam form Lake Mead, a popular spot for boating, water-skiing, and fishing.

Hoover Dam contains enough concrete to build a sidewalk, four-feet wide, around the earth's equator.

The Petrified Forest National Park is in northeastern Arizona. Logs that look like rocks are scattered everywhere. Two hundred million years ago, those logs were living trees. Then, the trees

Places to See in Arizona

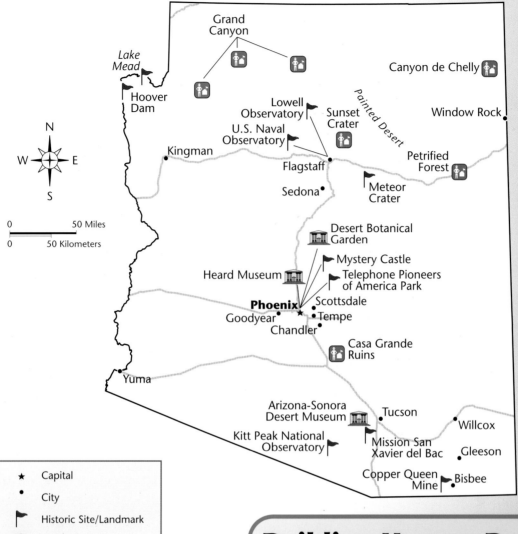

Grand Canyon

Lake Mead

Hoover Dam

Canyon de Chelly

Lowell Observatory

Sunset Crater

Painted Desert

Window Rock

U.S. Naval Observatory

Kingman

Petrified Forest

Flagstaff

Meteor Crater

Sedona

Desert Botanical Garden

Mystery Castle

Heard Museum

Telephone Pioneers of America Park

Phoenix

Scottsdale

Goodyear

Tempe

Chandler

Casa Grande Ruins

Yuma

Arizona-Sonora Desert Museum

Tucson

Willcox

Kitt Peak National Observatory

Mission San Xavier del Bac

Gleeson

Copper Queen Mine

Bisbee

Compass: N W E S

0   50 Miles
0   50 Kilometers

★ Capital

● City

⚑ Historic Site/Landmark

🏛 Museum

National Park/ Monument

died. Most trees decay when they die. Before these trees could decay, however, they were covered with mud and ash from ancient **volcanoes.** Over a long period time, the wood became petrified. That means it became as hard as stone.

Building Hoover Dam

Work began on Hoover Dam in 1931. It took 8,000 workers 5 years to finish the job. They spent the first year digging four tunnels, each as wide as a four-lane highway. When the tunnels were ready, the Colorado River flowed through them rather than along its riverbed. When the dam was finished in 1936, workers closed the tunnels, and the river returned to its original course.

Visitors to the Petrified Forest can touch the petrified logs. They are not, however, allowed to take any away with them.

The Petrified Forest is in the Painted Desert. This section of the Great Basin Desert runs south along the Little Colorado River. The Painted Desert got its name from the brightly colored rocks found there. Even the air over the Painted Desert is sometimes a light pink or purple from dust kicked up by wind.

West of the Petrified Forest, about halfway to Flagstaff, is Meteor Crater. About 50,000 years ago, a meteorite, a rock from space, slammed into the earth at 45,000 miles an hour. The space rock punched a hole, or crater, in the earth a mile across. The crater is the best preserved in the world.

Sunset Crater, northeast of Flagstaff, is another type of crater. It is the remains of a volcano that exploded 900 years ago. Its red sides rise 1,000 feet above the surrounding land. The best viewing is at sunset, thus the crater's name. The setting sun makes the red rock look like it is on fire.

Northern Arizona is filled with the ruins left by the Anasazi, particularly cliff dwellings. On the Navajo Reservation is Canyon de Chelly. The canyon holds some 400 Anasazi ruins. The most famous is the 60-room White House Ruins, named for its white plaster walls. It was once home to an entire village.

SOUTHERN ARIZONA

The Desert Botanical Garden is located in Phoenix, in southern Arizona. The garden has 20,000 plants, one of the most complete collections in the world. Although many of the plants are native to Arizona, particularly to the Sonoran Desert, the garden also has large numbers from other parts of the world.

Between Phoenix and Tucson are Hohokam remains, known as *Casa Grande,* Spanish for "big house." For 300 years, beginning around 1150, the Hohokam lived at Casa Grande. Some of the irrigation canals that they used to water their crops are still visible. Also still visible are parts of the seven-foot wall that surrounded the homes.

Today, people travel from all over to visit the ruins of Casa Grande. Historians are still unsure of the exact purpose of the building.

The Heard Museum is also in Phoenix. In 1929 Dwight and Maie Heard started the museum to house their personal collection of Native American art. In the years since, the collection has grown. The museum now has the largest collection of pieces from Southwestern Native American cultures, both ancient and modern. The museum also highlights the living cultures of Native Americans.

To the west of Tucson is the world-famous Arizona-Sonora Desert Museum. It is part museum and part zoo. There are displays showing such things as the inside of a saguaro or how scientists dig up and preserve fossils. At the heart of the museum are its living exhibits. All are native to the Sonoran Desert. The museum has more than 10,000 fish, hundreds of other animals, and thousands of plants.

No trip to Arizona would be complete without a tour of one of Arizona's 275 ghost towns. A ghost town is one that all or most of its citizens have left. Most of Arizona's ghost towns were mining settlements that died when the mines ran out of ore and the miners left. Gleeson, northeast of Bisbee, grew up around a copper strike in 1890. Most of its residents left in 1939 when the mines played out. Today visitors explore the ruins of the town hospital, study the remains of the jail, and walk through the town graveyard. They might even meet the two or three people who still call Gleeson home.

Father Eusebio Francisco Kino founded a Spanish mission known as San Xavier del Bac in what is now Tucson in 1701. The church is still in use today. Its white plaster walls that stand out against the blue Arizona sky and its peaceful aims have earned it the name "White Dove of the Desert." In 1990 workers began to clean and repair the mission so that it would appear as it had 300 years ago. Officials hired special artists to restore its many paintings and statues.

The current church of San Xavier was built from 1783 to 1797 by Fathers Juan Bautista Valderrain and Juan Bautista Llorenz.

Map of Arizona

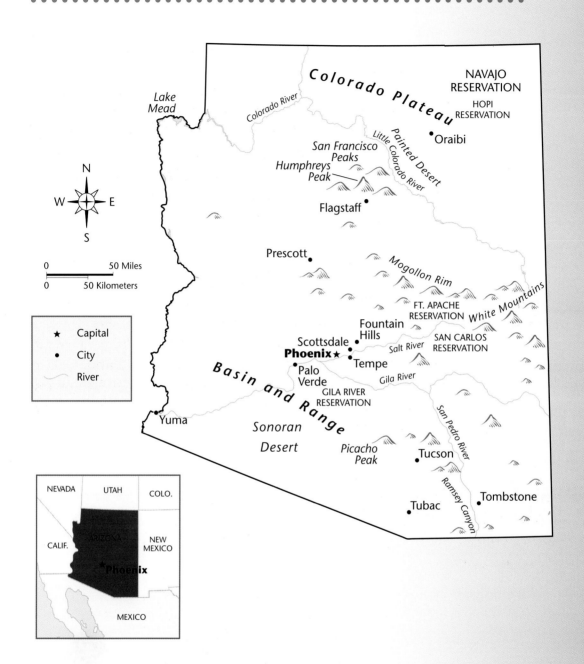

Lake Mead

Colorado Plateau

NAVAJO RESERVATION

HOPI RESERVATION

Colorado River

Oraibi

Painted Desert

Little Colorado River

San Francisco Peaks

Humphreys Peak

Flagstaff

N
W E
S

0   50 Miles
0   50 Kilometers

★ Capital
• City
〰 River

Prescott

Mogollon Rim

White Mountains

FT. APACHE RESERVATION

Fountain Hills

Scottsdale

Phoenix ★

Tempe

Salt River

SAN CARLOS RESERVATION

Palo Verde

Gila River

GILA RIVER RESERVATION

Basin and Range

San Pedro River

Yuma

Sonoran Desert

Picacho Peak

Tucson

Tubac

Ramsey Canyon

Tombstone

NEVADA   UTAH   COLO.

CALIF.   ARIZONA   NEW MEXICO

★ Phoenix

MEXICO

Glossary

atoms the smallest units of an element

attorney general chief law officer of a state or nation

bill a proposed law

boycott to refuse to buy a product or service as a protest

cactus a plant that stores water and protects itself with sharp spines

canyon an unusually deep and narrow valley with steep sides. Rivers may form canyons by cutting through the soft rocks of a dry region.

climate the usual weather of a place

civil suit a court action that involves the rights of private citizens. A civil suit may be brought to secure payment for an injury or damaged property.

Civil War the 1861–1865 conflict between the United States and eleven slave-holding southern states that wanted to form their own country

Confederacy the nation formed by eleven slave-holding southern states after breaking away from the United States in 1861

Democrat a member of the democratic political party, one of the two major U.S. political parties

drought a long period of dry weather. A drought may last for years.

elevation the height of the land. Elevation is often measured from sea level or the top of the ocean.

enchiladas rolled tortillas filled with meat and cheese and served with a sauce

endangered at risk of dying out

erosion the wearing away of soil by water or wind

felony a serious crime such as murder or burglary

fossil the remains of ancient plant or animal

irrigation to bring water to farmland through pipes, canals, and pipelines

marshals officers of the law who carry out court orders

mesa a flat-topped hill with steep sides

misdemeanor a minor crime such as disturbing the peace

missionary one who tries to convert others to his or her religion or beliefs

nuclear a type of energy that comes from splitting atoms into tiny particles

precipitation rain, snow, or sleet

pueblo a village or community with stone or clay buildings grouped around a central plaza

Republican a member of the republican political party, one of the two major U.S. political parties

resented to have felt angry about

reservations public lands set aside by the U.S. government for Native Americans

secretary of state public official responsible for keeping state records and the state seal

superintendent of public education public official responsible for a state's school system

strike the refusal of workers to stay on the job until their employer meets their demands

treasurer person in charge of the money of a government

veto to reject a bill passed by a legislature

volcano a mountain or opening in the earth that sends out lava, hot rocks, and gas

World War II the 1941–1945 war that the United States and its allies waged against Germany, Japan, and their allies

More Books to Read

• •

Bialy, Raymond. *The Navajo.* New York: Benchmark Books, 1999.

Moreillon, Judi. *Sing Down the Rain.* Walnut, Calif.: Kiva Publishing, 1997.

Standard, Carole K. *Arizona.* New York: Children's Press, 2002.

Thompson, Kathleen. *Arizona.* Austin, Tex.: Raintree/Steck-Vaughn, 1996.

Urban, William L. *Wyatt Earp: The O.K. Corral and the Law of the American West.* New York: PowerKids Press, 2003.

Index

About the Author

James A. Corrick has lived in Tucson, Arizona, for 30 years. He is the author of 25 books and 200 articles and short stories.